Don

Somewhere

For my friends

First published in 2009 by
DEADGOOD Publications
England

Copyright © Don Walls 2009. All rights reserved. No part of this publication may be reproduced, stored in a retrieval system, or transmitted, in any form or by any means, without the prior permission of the author.

Cover illustration by Don Walls

Also by Don Walls:
"In the Shed", published in 2005 (ISBN 978-9546937-1-8)
"Inside Out", published in 2006 (ISBN 978-9546937-4-9)
"Down the Lane", published in 2008 (ISBN 978-9546937-5-6)

Printed by Abbey Print, Hemingbrough, North Yorkshire, England

CONTENTS

Fireweed	1
My Uncle	2
Mr Martin	3
Ted - Window Cleaner	4
Tom the Horse	5
My First Girlfriend	6
The Deserter	7
The Jubilee	8
Romans - Bees	9
My Father	10
Guilt	11
my father's head	12
Bobby	13
The Mind of the Poet	14
The Poet and his Poems Drift Apart	15
On Reading Robert Frost's *Mending a Wall*	16
On Reading Stephen Spender's Poem, 'I think only of the truly great...'	17
Poetry	18
Love Poem	19
Dogs I have Known	20
There's always something going on	21
Water	22
Stones	23
Holidays	24
Carp	25
Weatherman	26
Eating Poetry	27
Mad About Geese	28
Pebbles	29
Grandma	30
Sometimes I saw them on the Ings	31
Meeting	32
Lesson	33
Thought Watching	34
Relationships	35
Snow	36
Weeds	37
Oh Lady!	38

CONTENTS (continued)

Clock	39
Buttons	40
Visual Puns	41
Adhesive par Excellence	42
Megalomania	43
Form	44
For an Artist who Talks to his Painting as he Paints	45
Mister Lovett	46
Personal Development	47
The Don Walls' Natural History Museum of Abstract Qualities	48
Us Curtains	49
Invisible	50
My Nose	51
The Autobiography of a Bookmark	52
Grief	53
My Pet Chicken	54
In the Pub	56
Tiger	57
Beast of a Meeting	58
Warthogs in York	59
Zip	60
The Points System	61
Monkey	62
this geezer	63
My Irony	64
Safari	65
Plant	66
Square	67
Courses	68
A few weeks ago I acquired a square that has five corners	69
Circus	70
Phone	71
My Recklessness	72
Bad Language	73
The Art of Trespass	74
Pythagoras	75
Wolf	76

Fireweed

I offer you fireweed
and you wrinkle your nose
though not much is left
when summer grows less
in the hedgerows
barren places by the road
the railway track
- greenness, redness
by the wood
along the dene
and whatever it is
we think we've seen
somewhere in the fireweed,

and when all that's left
is yellow grass
spine of foxglove
ice and snow,
I touch the glow upon your cheek
and remind you of the fireweed.

My Uncle

My only blood uncle
on my father's side
and we sat by the oak
- limbs rigid, knuckles gnarled,
each Winter a fossil
a green surprise each Spring
and he told me stories of fox and hare
and sky-blue eggs
and stroked the catkins, pussy willow
- daffodils,
spears in the darkening wind
and this boulder moored
to the brink of the hill
his face
my face on its face
brimming with stone stuff
- deaf to cuckoo bleat and moo
the blood buzz singing in our ears.

Mr Martin
(For Carol and Paul)

Professor-man
fingered moss on backyard walls
fetched groundsel, vetch
pressed specimens in his almanac
and from his trawling mac he dragged his gilded tome on British birds
- crows starlings - grey-lag geese honking north.
'Oh tell us of the north,' we said, wellied-cold on Arctic nights
and beneath the gas lamp light in our street he shambled bears
on ice floes bigger than Clifton Ings
warned melting at the polar caps would drown us all
swirl water round our chimney stacks.

Beetles - we eyed them through his lens - mites, ants
the fur coat of the bumble bee, thorax of wasp
spiders in cracks
white webs in Spring.
Beetles iridescent-backed
and whatever crawled he classified
told us how the housefly fed, syphoning nutrient in the rotting sun
and how beneath the floorboards of each house
the prehistoric cockroach multiplied.

Horses - he stroked the Clydesdale that fetched our coal
checked it for tics
and hummed the classics
and living next door was the only audience I ever had
as I fudged Scarlatti on the piano.
Once he gave me a threepenny bit.

But oh to be with him on a starlit night,
amazed at the thought that stars extinct lit up the sky.
We stared at Venus and traced the Plough.
'Somewhere out there on a planet like ours there're folk,' he said,
'a Mr Martin even staring at stars.'
I couldn't imagine another Mr Martin anywhere.

Ted - Window Cleaner

Biggest fibber this side of the Ouse.
Cleaner of royal windows, he claimed
- once at the palace it started to rain
when the late king raised a window and said,
'Ted, tha'll catch thee death o' cold
come in until it stops
and have a cup of tea.'

Purveyor of knowledge
- Ted knew our lane from end to end
downfall pipes and rotten gutters
the Johnson's Duckett, the Smith's lovely lav
why Linda Lane had gone away, stayed with grandma in farthest Kent
and on his rounds he always found what was lost
Tom Smart's marbles, my conker 94 years old,
the Spivey's cat.

He knocked at doors for water, talk -
drawn out, long, like the slow goods train on the Scarborough line;
three windows in an afternoon, not more,
he knew no time,
'til evening sent him home for lack of light,
then humping his ladder down the lane
met Mrs White fetching clips for tomorrow's rugs.
Oh then he'd talk the moon around
while his missus kept warm his fish and chips.

Late November, 1948 Ted fell from his ladder and broke his neck.
The neighbours dropped in to pay respects,
Ted laid out in the dim front room.
They all came out
awed at the silence that surrounded him.

Tom the Horse

When Ken came to jog round the field
Tom, the horse, jumped around like a foal
nuzzled his back, neighed,
trotted behind him.

One morning, after heavy rain, Tom sank in the beck
- bellows of breath
and Ken came running with ropes and belts
- the mud sucking back -
and stroking his head eased him forward
word by word
and Tom spluttered and snorted.
The squelching release, Ken's arms round his neck.

Then the diptheria epidemic '39
and I went down to the field
Tom standing there
mane in the wind
and he stared for days over the hedge - ears pricked,
jumped around sometimes, like a foal.

My First Girlfriend

She packed chocolates at Rowntree's
and I waited for her by the clock
and walked her home.
(My other love snooker
the geometry of knowing
where the balls would go.)
Saturday nights - the Grand
and once we saw a western twice.

Sundays - the Ings,
the litter of fox cubs
quails in the wind
and the orchid which no one else would ever see
- purplish pink.
The strange ferns of frost.

That Monday I waited by the clock
'til the lamp lighter came.

At home, the note in the letter box.
I jumped on my bike
and furiously pedalled
round the block
and never went to the Ings again,
played snooker seriously,
every night.

The Deserter

Jason, my uncle
pushed ladders high, stammered
shouldered tree trunks, bricks
rescued a cat from the Johnson's roof
warmed day-old chicks
and waited for the owl to glide
land on the larch at the garden's end.

Then the war - called up -
no news for weeks
and at the front door, the back
police
and grandad's words about deserters on the Somme.
I couldn't sleep
and once past midnight the backyard sneck.

Questioned on my way to school
weathered glances down the street,
silence in the corner shop.

Then early April, the smoky crow
cobbles still wet
boots and voices down the lane
police, redcaps
and they flushed him out of the Johnson's shed.
Men grimaced, leaning on bikes.
Wives came out.

The Jubilee

His wife smiling
- her jar of beans
raffle tickets - a floppy giraffe
his sermon on the Jubilee
then, down to the church
- weddings, funerals for the coming week -
and Shirty White and Stalky and me
wandered aimless - coconuts darts
guessing the weight of Tom Smith's marrow
'til boredom suggested
we went to the church.

In the half light of silence
we tiptoed in
incense lingering from Sunday's service,
the alter piece - the threadbare angels -
and we peeped through the crack in the vestry door
Shirty first then Stalky, then me
- a jolt of guilt
and we wondered what Miss White would think
but a curious excitement kept us focused.
Then Shirty again, then Stalky then me
- a long last peep and the blush unseen
at my trespass into someone's life.

The glow of red windows - the failing light
and back in the street
'How lovely,' he said, 'the day has been'
his wife still smiling - her jar of beans
and I glanced at Miss White
and wondered what words and meaning meant.

Romans - Bees
(As a child, my thoughts never hovered for long, flitting seamless from one thing to another on a subtle logic that kept them in flight. In the time dimension events overlap).

Kids - we learned about the Romans
cohorts from France crossing the Channel
helmets, breast plates - standards and eagles
and at the end of the garden my father's bees
- the crescendo of swarming -
the mid day sun - the heat of armour on our backs
bees foraging - foxglove, clover
and the chant of marching
- Eboracum, Lindinium
bees settling in the copper sun
hornets plundering
- hedgerows of fear
and bees on their backs
feet in the air
Romans frozen
Mithras - ice winds
and huddling in camps
'til the sun's first glance
and the bees coming back
furred and mumbling.

My Father

A covering of snow just hanging on
and my father digging
- clabber, clay
and the frosts coming back, their wedges of ice

and he heaved and sliced
and stretched a line
to keep me straight

a mound of soil on the palm of his hand,
smelling its sweetness
as if this were the first Spring
before the Spring of weeds and crocus.

Guilt

It goes back to the Johnson's orchard
and me and Mick nicking apples,
blushing lies and swigging cider in Tom Smythe's shed,
flattening ha'pennies to pennies on the line at night,
smoking twist and cinnamon sticks,
my under age pint in the Golden Ball
and the elbow mentality of pushing folk out
and getting ahead

and then the war
- a no man's land of opposing beliefs
love thy neighbour and kill the Germans
and God on our side guilt was absolved
but you could never pretend it wasn't there
it fed on desire to nourish itself
and desire was everywhere
gambling for fags,
Sharon's boobs, Millie's legs.

my father's head
(for Emma)

my dad's head
has five sides the top the back the front two sides
but where the other side should be
- his neck his chin
the front is crowded
eyes and things
but the back is empty
I don't know why
I like the way his nose turns up
but up it is not very nice
his mouth's alright
but his head is bald
it can't stay underwater long
everything should do something
but his eyebrows don't do anything
his forehead is for frowning with

Bobby

The Joneses kept cats from the beginning of time,
bedraggled, dripping, stinking cats.
Prehistoric monster cats that howled and shagged to the ends of the earth
Bobby the worst werewolfed, mangled, raped and pissed,
shit in Mrs McCumber's window box, 'Poisoned all my plants,' she said

'not our Bobby,
our Bobby wouldn't would our Bobby
- Bobby wouldn't hurt a bird,'
droned Mrs Jones
and the bugger purred.

The Mind of the Poet
(For Antonia and Steve)

At a soirée (the intellectuals there)
Larkin sat in the Georgian window
outside delphiniums
roses glowed
Larkin lost in a world of flowers, inside
the evening soared on wings of wine,
Hughes and Heaney
and some glanced his way as if to invite him to join in
but the poet was preoccupied
with plants and things across the lawn
'til on the ebbtide of the evening
he shifted his focus to the world inside.

The room was silent.

Then, Larkin spoke
'I've finally worked out'
he said to his host
'where you keep the rubbish bins.'
And then he walked out.

The Poet and his Poems Drift Apart

Larkin: his slim volume
- poems going where I've never been:
Church Going, Weddings, An Arundel Tomb
- the truth in each verse of a testy old fart,
the poet and his poetry drift apart.

Apple Picking - Frost -
and I touch the apples in each line
- verse clear as ice,
birches springing in the thaw of March
irascible, tetchy,
poet and poems drift apart.

And Wantling getting through to the real and true
in the harshness of verse,
'Fuck me, I'm a poet,' he said
a poet fucked up with a singing heart,
poet and poetry drift apart.

On Reading Robert Frost's *Mending a Wall*
(For Carol)

What the ice has done to walls
the rain has done to wood
and there's a thud of hammers down the backs
to get things right before the Spring
and some bring their deeds to prove a point:
an injudicious post, a tree that's grown beyond itself,
a tongue of shade that wraps around the neighbour's flowers
- each garden an island to itself.

Between me and my neighbour Sue next door, there's a gap in the hedge
and she borrows milk and I borrow sugar
and if I'm ill, she walks straight in
and never stays too long, or little
- our fences made of subtler stuff
than brick and wood.

On Reading Stephen Spender's Poem,
'I think only of the truly great...'

I think of those who, never in the public gaze,
sing of love, kindling fires in fading lives

keeping vigil over those who only dimly understand
and those who do and question why

and all whose reverential hands
quietly tend what's left of life, or
life that never blooms.

I think of those whose presence fills the air with blossom,
their gentle unremembered words,

yet they are truly heirs of greatness
evolution refined to spirit,
singing endless down the ages.

Poetry
(Inspired by Damien Hurst's chopped up cow in formaldehyde)

Since there's some debate
on what contemporary poetry is
I've published a poem in formaldehyde
you can see it in the Modern Tate,

chopped into stanzas
you'll see how it works
- physiology of rhyme
structure of bones
its tone and style
and cadence of flesh

and in turn with the turn
the Arts are taking (the Turner Prize)
I've made the poem come alive
recite itself and tap a dance.

The curious queues stand amazed.
'But is this poetry?' someone asks.

Love Poem

I took my dog and therapist for a walk
and offered her bouquets of Yorkshire mist
sorrel, vetch.
She planted daisies in my beard
and like a child
pushed buttercups almost
up my nose.
My dog explored the summer-long grass.
A partridge whirred
then over the hill
dandelions in the flowering sun
- she fetched them in armfuls
and my dog ran in circles unravelling scents
and we lay among clocks, thousands rising in the air.

Dogs I have Known

Tail whirling
he growled and howled
and how could a dog howl so much sound?
They heard, they say, his grand aggression in Cromer Street,
streets away
- this dog that put the wind up dads
licked our hands.
Floss his name, Tiger to us lads.

Patch
A mean and mangy flea-bitten dog
- no one entered his domain.
He chewed the curtains, gnawed chair legs
mounted bitches down the lane,
for prowess males
or someone's leg.

Flash
The gentlest dog I've ever known
take his bone he never growled.
Beneath a fringe of Beardie hair his pleading eyes.
He nosed your hand,
a huge warm hearthrug of a dog.
No fuss.
When his time had come he just made off.

A priest once said,
'A dog has no place in the Kingdom of God.'
Tiger, Patch - their glowering eyes
and even Flash
would see him off in paradise.

There's always something going on

There's always something going on
- a few grains here, pools there
mutual intrusions
- water deep inland
and out at sea islands, spits
shingle settling where I stand
- currents, winds - the vaccilation of sand.

Water

Illusionist -
now it's here now it's not
- dew on the grass
pools on the path
(if only I could appear, disappear like that)
and nothing's closer than water
the closest of closeness
- the oldest of tricks
two drops on the window
lost in each other,

and my hand in the water
this side of the lake
in the same water the other side of the lake.

Stones
(For Kay and John)

Sometimes I surprise a brood of them
under the alder,
their round vowels lipping the silence.

Artists in moss and weather,
articulate in frosts
the sun's long glare
- my mind wandering off
pre Cambrian, Cretacious,
- incredulous, they stare.

Holidays

I'm tired of the holiday hassle
you can spend your holidays abroad, at home
paddle in the bath and surf your thoughts
- travel by thought is real enough:
Ibiza and the South of France
and take excursions on Park and Ride
close your eyes and paraglide,
cross the Ouse as you'd cross the Channel
speak French in Poppleton
and ride your bike on the right-hand side
- if stopped by the law simply say
je suis étranger.
At night, your pillow's a sanctuary - white
on some arid road in Greece, by the sea,
thoughts swaying as sleep drifts in.

Carp

I stood in the water.
Carp - deep-bellied
still
- the underwater floating
huge and ancient,
quiet fins stirring
and one raised his head
and stared at me
breathing white,
his autumn colours
russet bronze
underbelly white
- water muttering
round my feet.

Weatherman

I store weather in my head
and turn on sunlight, garden rain.
Also at Christmas, guiltily though, I bet on snow
then unleash blizzards
and for cussedness, sometimes, I burst the clouds.

I love crispy autumns
and crazy springs,
buds bursting everywhere
- whiteness and the flaky air,

and manic sometimes
I could wake the world to searing ice
shivering suns
and floods to drown the Minster towers
- a biblical raining of frogs and pigs
squealing in the rising air.

Eating Poetry

For starters a haiku
and for the main course - a sonnet or ode,
I like what's organic
- free range, free verse
      poems diverse
but some are too fat
and some are scraggy
nothing but bones
and rhyme, sometimes, gets stuck in my throat,

if a poem's nutritious, I pick it clean
and once I wolfed an epic down,
it gave me wind,

traditional - blank verse for Sunday lunch
for dessert a lyric
and for a night out terza rima, sestina
dactyls, trochee

and for supper
quatrains, jingles
doggerel, ditties
comic verse
burlesque and limericks
- the inbred need for rhythm, rhyme.

Mad About Geese
(Ways of seeing)

My wife can't stand them
- raucous, hiss,
but me I adore them
my fantasy wild beguiled by geese,

they teach me to fly
*adjust my flap, my neck, my span
and train me to honk
on the mud flats late at night
'I'm a natural,' they say
and invite me to the Tundra chill,*
then wheel beyond the harbour wall
and out to sea

and you have to admire their will of wings
arching the oceans
their curious energy stirring the air.

Through the long dry Summer each morning at dawn
I long for geese touching down
and crank my honk to flying pitch
- my wife chunters something
about old Christmas dinners,
paté de foie gras
and buries her head in the goose down pillow.

Pebbles

You find them everywhere
- rivers, moors
but mostly on beaches

singing shanties,
round blind songs in pinks and blues
and for certain they know you'll pick them up
- you can't resist it
smoothness - cold, on the palm of your hand.

Grandma

as if remembering
were a duty like
going to church or
saying prayers
I remembered
every day
at first
'til days slipped into
weeks

weeks

months then
out of mind and
put away in
rooms up
stairs like
stuff no longer used

but
recently
she's come to light
me on her knee
her whispering
we'll go to Scarborough on a train
come spring

Sometimes I saw them on the Ings
- lark and warbler,
the strange dance of grebes.

Down the lane whisperings.
Her father lived in the backyard shed.
Her mother shopped streets away
and no one dropped in
- the vicar once.

Nights, I glimpsed her putting the milk jug out
her satin gown,
at the curtains sometimes
like something startled in the wood.
Then Mrs White and the lights on all night.

Early Spring - the slates still wet
I saw her in the lane again
- speech aborted

and once on the Ings
- islands of mud,
every step a squelch.

Meeting

Parking in the forecourt - a few flakes floating -
an old fox stared at me
and seemed to wonder who I was
and where I was going
- an old fox - silver backed with Winter closing in.

He slipped through the hedge
then suddenly was back
as if our meeting had been too brief.
I held out my hand
and spoke to him.
He nosed the air, his paw raised slightly above the ground
- the sound of leaves, the wind.

Lesson

I look outside.
Sunlight greens the Winter boughs
of beech, facing south,
a gull rides the air
in perfect hyperbola. Inside,
Stephen manoeuvres round the table
and David, Robert
strive to co-ordinate
forms on paper - a triangle,
parallel lines. Diane's green
overflows her drawing of a tree
and someone stammers, 'C - Christmas soon.'

Outside, the sunlight shifts to evening,

a hand rests gently
on Ronnie's shoulder.
Light falls across their pictures on the walls,
Kay's green eyes.

Thought Watching

My head is a marvellous place
for watching thoughts.
They appear at any time
just strolling along or walking the dog.

With each other, some wrestle for days
- I have a ringside seat.
Others like birds skitter on snow,
their tracks soon covered
and some of them drive me from my head
or fetch me a poem

- and all the thoughts that keep me alive:
the tilt of the moors
and frost in the heather Kilburn to Wass,
your sense of direction
and both of us lost.

Weeds

Chop them down and overnight they're back again
their expertise hanging on.
They maraud like goths, visigoths
and never give in
to all the pests the sky rains down
or canker of roots
and poisoned even, effete for months,
their green horns pierce the earth again
and they bloom sometimes
tiny flowers - whites and blues
and this too is a stratagem
and you're disinclined to wrench them out
and soon the gravel is sprouting them
so you leave it to Winter to freeze them out,
but early Spring they rise again
first the sortie, then the attack.

Oh Lady!

If only I could take her
and shake her out of her elegant self
and say 'Look lass, cut out the cocktail crap, woman your speech
with the woman you are.'

'Why all this pose, this wish to be Queen,
this delicate embroidery on the air?
Unstitch unravel - the thread's all wrong,
I'd rather have you naked as you are.

Scowl my days and dagger with hate
but oh lady not your smiles
silvered out of nothing on the air,
for greenness sake
grow back to what I know you are.

Wrench out the tongue of dainty speech
damn the demure, perfume of status, manner, rank
and do it quick before you have forgotten who you are.'

Clock

My job's to remind them
from the alarm early morning to the midnight news,
but nothing's simple
- I run forward sometimes or lag behind
and they glance at me in disbelief
and to suit the sun
adjust me one hour
every Autumn, Spring,
but there's something more
their sense of time, not mine,
relative to tears, love
- slowing me down or pushing me forward.

Buttons

There ought to be a Union for buttons.
We have no rights,
kept like strays in old biscuit tins
and only noticed if we're hanging off,
or lost, but we have our pride in buttoning up,
and style:
pearly on shirts,
brilliant on guards
or left unbuttoned above the bosom on a lady's blouse,
as if unplanned.
Since braces went out we're redundant on trousers,
no longer on flies and fewer on cuffs.
The old communities are breaking up.
If we went on strike they'd hire zips or velcro.

Visual Puns

Your wit Picasso
flicks from handlebars and bicycle seat
to Iberian bull
like Dali's Narcissus
holding a stone between finger and thumb

flicks, I say - bull or bike,
perceptions tipped one way or the other.
(Who shall I marry Jill or Jane
John or Mike?)

and nothing's certain
like Dali's Voltaire
- at the blink of an eye two nuns are there.

Adhesive par Excellence

I am a practitioner in it
it works on everything - homes hearts,
but you have to be careful -
double check the parts before application.

Once mending two marriages
I cemented the wrong folk
though coupling was strong - better than most
(pairing like this could come into vogue).

Shrinks are manic about it
especially for breakdowns, personality splits,
and the pedant uses it to actually fix infinitive splits,
but there are of course, difficult cases:
the smithereens of lives and pots
and promises present a special case
- first, folk rarely admit that one's been broken,
so our latest glue cements a promise as soon as it's spoken.
(Politicians are debating the implications of this).

Megalomania

Once upon a time there was a circle
- a pure continuum of himself
no beginning no end
and he saw himself in everything:
the moon, the earth, the howling of wolves
and the subtle roundness that informs the Arts
and all that's cyclic - birth and death.
'Whatever's round is complete,' he said,
'God is complete, therefore God is round.'

Form

To pour one's poetry in a mould
of stanzas, rhymes and metric lines
a means of making sense conform
to all devices artifice defines
implies a sacrifice in sense
unless the sense creates the form.

For an Artist who Talks to his Painting as he Paints

Here words meet texture, subtlety of colour.
Deep in the subsoil, gutterals of oak
mutterings of leaves
and his brush murmurs 'Summer'
syllables ascending - bee-buzz, lark
dark sometimes, flapping like crows
blackthorn, tits, magpies garrulous
and patches unpainted - wordless, quiet.

Mister Lovett

Mister Lovett - master of clichés
once at a meeting he nodded off,
and through the channels of sleep
someone asked 'And what do you think, Mr Lovett?'
Cliché quick his answer was
'It all depends on how you look at it
at this moment in time,
with a global view
in real terms too'

'Let us be clear,' he said,
'for the sake of the record,'
and he addressed all problems he'd taken on board.

A man of faith was Mr Lovett
'Life,' he said 'has a hidden agenda,
at the end of the day
on a level playing field
I'll meet my maker.'

Personal Development
(For Tracy and Michael)
(This poem was inspired by the proliferation of bizarre courses
- especially those of a pseudo-scientific nature)

I'm teaching a course on how to hold a cocktail glass,
wine glass and other receptacles for social drinking
from martinis to kvass.

Classes weekly Canon Lee,
I have a Master's, a PhD
and receive commendations from students worldwide,

this from Miss B:
I'm simply amazed
how holding the glass with the pinky raised
has changed my life. I endorse your course,

and this from John Lee:
I was a nobody at work,
nights out with the staff
but after your class - gestures and the glass
I imbibe with style,
I've just been promoted - clerk first class.

As for Miss Lyle:
my firm and seductive grasp of the glass
has galvanized my life of sex,
I'd like to sign on for your course next term
on 'Pouting while Drinking.' I enclose my cheque.

And next year a syllabus brand new!
There are a few in the States
but from market research, there's a need here too,
so Friday week, 3pm we're holding a taster at the Chase
on 'Picking your Nose with Elegance, Grace.'

The Don Walls' Natural History Museum of Abstract Qualities

Room I - suddenness,
bounding like a rabbit
from a darkening wood.

Loops - Room II - tinged red,
wound by swallows
round the evening sky.

Something sensitive scenting the air
- Room III,

and I was surprised.
I exhibit my surprise
- Room IV.

Room V - Silence
from the North York Moors,
slightly holed by songs of birds.

Room VI
- all the love I've found
through the long grass of years.

Us Curtains

We block out the light while they're watching TV
let in the morning
shut out the night
and shut in all the little things:
eyeing their age in a full length mirror
- belly, baldness, conducting the concert on Radio 3
and nothing's different down the street,
our perennial screening
hiding love and what they're eating.

Invisible

Invisible one morning, I confirmed in the mirror I wasn't there,
cock-a-hoop slipped everywhere
lives of celebrities, millionaires
and I could have reported for the Mirror, the Sun
- barefaced facts on scandalous affairs.
Everyone I nosied out - neighbours friends,
with the visceral excitement of finding out
what's from the heart
what's doctrinaire
in a shadowy world of cause and effect
assumption and fact
but, being invisible never lasts
and I see myself in the bedroom mirror slipping back
with the burden of knowing
what means what
and who loves who
and who does not.

My Nose

It has a front seat
(squinty, I glimpse it)
sebaceous shines
- craters, zits.
Its effluent ineffable.

Saddled with glasses
and once a pince-nez in Drury Lane,
sun cream in Crete.
Wonders what might have been:
the thingamabob, ringed to the septum
diamante inlaid,
nose job.
Savours the perfumes of herbs and roses
wrinkles at sweat
anything malodorous,
adores warm bread, fresh sheets,
lingers sometimes in a cloud of Chanel.
Smells memories:
Christmas dinners down the lane,
the corridors at school
- Ajax and Jane.

The Autobiography of a Bookmark

I was cradled in stories happily ending
spent school-long-years in grammar inviolable
chanting tables, then Penthouse and Playboy,
bibled through gospels, King James' version
- almost converted by the lilt of words.
Survived years of tedium in King's Regulations.
How refreshing to lie in the language of Shakespeare
Keats and Wordsworth
as one might lie in the freshness of grass.

Out of work in the 80s - part time pages,
directories, almanacs - nothing secure,
and close to black print all my dog-eared life
I'm wary of words
singing in poetry
or hunting in packs
and I dream of white margins,
quiet paths between lines.

Grief

In the garden that night
the news came through
- me in her rocking chair, writing a poem
rhythm, rhyme
and the rocking chair stopped before the end of a line.

I kicked it, smashed it against the wall
flung arms and legs on the fire
- it crackled and spat,
and the poem ... the poem flared up
- syllables of sparks in the dark.

My Pet Chicken

I have a pet chicken - a warrior chicken,
wattles blood red.
She squawks at crows
and once she pecked a dog to death.
Cats yowled off
and kids dropped round
for gore and stuff
and we sat on the step my chicken and I
and pecked around some thoughts together
- what to clobber and what to not.

Braveheart girl,
head-hunted by the M.O.D.,
guest at Windsor, Lambeth, Chequers
leapt Ascot hats and umbrellas

spontaneous girl,
though I have to say a bit uncouth
shit on Dukes and Saville suits,

yawped and strutted and showed no fear
my gallant girl,
my Bodicea.

REQUESTS

In the Pub

Unlike me, Mary can chat to anyone
like last week in the Punch Bowl
there in the snug, a large white rabbit
drinking a bottle of Mackeson stout and smoking a pipe.

Mary recognised him straight away
- the driver on the Harrogate train
and after pleasantries about the weather
the conversation grew in depth -
'I'm Catholic,' the rabbit said
'got scores of kids.'
I looked at Mary as if to say
next he'll say 'I'm having a vasectomy.'

'I'm having a vasectomy,' the rabbit said.

At this point a man came in with a Jack Russell on a lead
- a little frenzied dismembered thing.
The rabbit left to drive his train.
Mary's ears stood erect,
she twitched her nose.

Tiger

I am a tiger.
I prowl and growl,
Saturday nights I go down town
leave my scent in clubs and bars
and spray the flowers in the parks
and anyone I do not like
- passers-by adore my stripes,
before first light I lollop home
my wife is mumbling at the door
- her fiery eyes, her throaty grr
I roll on my back and gently purr.

Beast of a Meeting

It lumbers in
has an agenda to keep it on track,
likes to be stroked,
its minutes read back,
feels its way forward dragging its feet
flops with fatigue,
covered in clichés
like burrs in the grass
grunts, repeats
eats acres of verbiage to nourish itself.
And then, it craps.

Warthogs in York

'We're going on safari,' Mary said,
'There're warthogs in York.
You can hear them when the traffic stops late at night'
and she donned her Harrods' safari jacket
with Mammals of Africa in her pocket
and led me to the centre of York,

and the rain it drizzled and the cold invaded my sheepskin coat
and at the entrance to the Roman Baths
I dared to ask, 'Is this the habitat for warthogs love?'
and Mary eyed me with bleak derision
and we scoured the shadows down the ginnels.
The cold was creeping up my back
- no longer could I feel my toes
so to bring the safari to a close,
down Back Swinegate
in the shadows, 'I think I've seen one love,' I said.
Unimpressed she read the language of my body
(she had an NVQ in this)
and also said, 'With negative thoughts and lagging behind
you'll never see a warthog love in York,'
and delivered a homily on positive thinking.
Then, I followed her down the streets of York - alleyways, ginnels
to Clifford's Tower where the Foss flows by the Pay and Display.
There Nature summoned
and beneath the birch and sapling trees
I'd just unbuttoned when I heard the squeal and grunt of pigs
- the rooting in the mush of leaves,
the porcine rush and glint of tusks
and bristles brushing my trouser legs.
They bowled me over in the mud,
their snouts in my pockets
(they must have smelt the Trebor mints).
Then squealing mad, they scampered off
and Mary quickly on the scene smiled and said:
'How positive love you must have been
so close to Warthogs in the city of York.'
She read the language of my body.

Zip

It's strange how folk return to their roots.
I, for example, have gone back to buttons
after struggling with zips for fifty years.
As a young man, I opted for progress in the name of zips
but there were teething problems from the start
and still are: the zipper refuses to ride on the teeth
and grips like a bulldog the puckered lining, so you can't zip up
and you can't zip down and sweltering in the noonday heat
you yank and tug in a zip-rage frenzy.
Once, imprisoned up to my neck, they scissored me free.
And once in midwinter my zipper zipped easily from bottom to top
but the coat flapped open.
What's more, if it doesn't work, you believe it's your fault
reinforced by your wife with a 'Come here, you hold it like this'
and she sides with the zip. Would you believe it?
Zipping up, of course, ought to carry a safety warning:
one morning a millidentured aggressive zip
gripped my penis by the neck
and held it like a rabbit, limp
(zips should be hunted on safari)
and from that day I returned to buttons
aesthetic in shape, colour, even touch.
Moreover, they work.

The Points System

To encourage my wife I give her points
- never too many
in case she thinks they're not worth having.
She uses them mainly
to cancel a batch of minus points acquired at night:
on my legs her icy feet
- pillow patter
when I want to sleep.
She drags the sheets and by day her misdemeanours grow
wrinkling her nose at what I say
and more cutting than words could ever be
that look that says 'I told you so,'
so her minus total grows and grows

For her birthday sometimes
I give her a point,
at Christmas, too,
and for this and that half a point
and if she scowls I take it back.
I never give her points in Lent.

Monkey
(For Chris and Peter)

That day Mary took me to see
her secret gargoyle in the Minster wall
that no one but her had ever seen.
'Up there,' she said, 'Don't take your eyes off it.'
Her peremptory tone kept me focused on the beast in stone
when suddenly it twitched and blinked its eyes.
It scratched its belly, armpits, toes.
It scratched its nose.
It scratched its crotch
and I closed and opened both my eyes
to check my vision was intact.
'It's a monkey,' I gasped.
'Ceropithecoid,' Mary said
- 'an old world anthropoid in Yorkshire stone.'
Then the beast swung down
and fed from her hand - peanuts, pistachios, a Trebor mint
and they chattered in Simian
when suddenly the monkey leapt back to its niche
and posed a pose of a gargoyle grave
as down the path tourists came
- French, German, Japanese
and I was about to apprise them of the beast
when a glance from Mary aborted speech.

Statue-still we stood against the Minster wall.

this geezer

this geezer like
woke up one morning and noticed
a leak in the roof of his head
where the cortex was damp
so he placed a bucket
beneath the drip
and called the shrink
who examined the ceiling
and plaster for cracks when suddenly
this geezer always a bit philosophical like
said isn't it odd we're both in one head
and the shrink he flipped

My Irony

My wife won't have him in the house
and locks him in the garden shed
though now and again I let him out
and words of praise are used to blame
- great is crap
sane is mad
and sometimes it's hard to tell
what's ironic and what is not
and what means what
as antonyms proliferate
and speaking straight
is almost dead,
so she locks him back in the garden shed.

Safari

Mary said a tiger lives in the shadows round St. Samson's Square.
Once she saw him after dark.

So, late November late at night
when the mists hung heavy and Rowntree's cocoa flavoured the air
we went on safari to the centre of York.

Crossing the Ouse we followed scent marks down the ginnels
Parliament Street, St. Samson's Square
where, in the shadows of the church,
the scent of tiger filled the air
and Mary gently coaxed him out
with gingerbread men and Pontefract cakes
and poured him milk in a china saucer.
The beast, adagio, sat down before her
his eyes on fire
his tail atwitch
he roared a roar fortissimo,
then wrapped himself in shadows again,

and Mary fed me gingerbread men
Pomfrey cakes
and huddling closer in the mists
poured my coffee in a saucer.

Plant

I have a pet plant
indulge him with a Chinese pot
and walk him round the Ings at night and round the block.
He sits beside me at the Proms
adores Bruckner Liszt
- poet physicist
loves wintry light and how light bends
- space, time
quantum leaps and paradigms.
I've introduced him to my friends
loquacious in The Old Grey Mare.
He's learnt to swear
takes everything in
my wife is not endeared to him,
so I keep him in the garden shed
but for goodwill on shivering nights
I let him in.
My wife won't have him near the bed.

Square

I stand four-square
my reputation angles, area.

There's no mistaking who I am
- my form is constant
a banker, businessman,

but one of these days
I'll bend at the knees and become a rhombus
or abandon area altogether

and my sides will wander
each its own way
and sway with the reeds,
the wild savannah.

Courses
(For Jane)

I've been on courses:
Work Introduction when work was rare as cod in the Ouse
- CVs CVs - every course I've been on I've written CVs,
and manage my time on paper at least.
Job Satisfaction and Marketing Skills
and Surfing on Adrenalin.
The Staff as a Team with Japanese speakers,
Rocking the Boat and Getting the Sack.
You and Your Boss.
Stress and Avoiding it.
Assessing Yourself and more CVs.
Managing Aggression at Home and Work.
Positive Thinking:
course upon course
my thinking unswerving
- courses are crap.

A few weeks ago I acquired a square that has five corners
the first rare square I've ever owned.
Also a triangle with two right angles.
Both free range, they walk around the garden lawn
at dusk, at dawn, on the Ings at night.

They have the most endearing features
polite, well-bred
but oh so shy
they hide behind the garden shed.
They're lovely creatures.

Circus
(For Matthew)

My mind a circus.
I am the performer in my head,
the ringmaster too.
I crack my whip, announce the acts
and from the wings they tumble in.

I swing from thoughts without a net,
juggle one low on fire sometimes
and throw one higher than the rest.

High in the big top I'm at my best
somersault, leap - balance on air,
wild thoughts snarling late at night
their fiery eyes, their tiger stripes.

I crack my whip
but there's always one that won't lie down,
I never turn my back on him.

Thank God there's a clown - a clown in my head
bulbous nose
sausage lips
flip flops, trips
walks a tightrope flat on the ground
climbs safe heights on imaginary steps.

Phone

My wife and family on the phone
- verbal effluent flooding the house
and the gritty unease of leaving a message
and speaking to no one.
Calls from India, Bangladesh,
cheaper gas and Everest
and worst of all the press button madness
and music you don't want to hear,
the abrupt interruption -
'Thanks for your patience you're still in the queue'
and you bang down the phone
and come back later
later and later
and the only word spoken is *shit* to yourself.

My Recklessness

Reckless from an early age,
I bet all my marbles on outspitting Tom Smythe,
swam the Ouse in flood.
Then the war and we tugged incendiaries from the mud
but most daring of all (in P.E.) -
lying down flat
bet on the length of Miss Brown's drawers
and more:
years chatting up the opposite sex
my studies a wasteland of neglect
and my verse I wrote in company time
but work and poetry didn't rhyme,
I got the sack.

So, I keep my recklessness in the garden shed,
but without him life's a one way street
so now and again I let him out
and you feel the excitement stirring your bowels,
'Up sticks,' he shouts
'Impress the chicks and get tattooed'
'Rave'
'Get wed.'

On this latter advice, I lock him back in the garden shed.

Bad Language

I keep my bad language in the garden shed.
You'd be surprised how many words it knows.
My wife won't have it in the house
and the neighbours keep their windows closed
when I exercise it on the garden lawn.

At night I walk it on the Ings when no one's there.
It gets much vulgarity off its chest
and I'm told it's the only bad language that's kept in a shed
though I've heard it too in little lean to's down the street.

A month ago the experts came to check it out
and pronounced it authentic when it pursed its mouth in a fricative 'f'
and told them to go.

At night sometimes I sit with it and learn a lot
- all its plosives, b's and p's
and for denouncing tommyrot
bullshit, bollocks

- so much abuse but kindness too:
'poor sod,' even love in 'little bugger.'

The Art of Trespass

I've published books on it:
The Chameleon Knack
maps, slides
chapter by experienced guides
luxury copy
morocco - hard back.

You can try all sorts of trespass with it
Big Ben
Balmoral, Lambeth
Number Ten
also chapter on covering one's tracks
- snow, loam,
stately homes.

The barbed wire syndrome
and gaps in the hedge,
relieving oneself
gender - stealth.

Trespass Advanced
- proceeding with grace,
personal space and crossing it.

Pythagoras
(For Alison)

Unswerving squares
in a world absurd
where A loves B
and B loves C
and C is gay anyhow
and all this squared.

And so Pythagoras,
I love to affirm your magic again
since out of disharmony to the power 'n'
your theorem proves that two sides squared
equal the square on the hypotenuse.

Wolf

I prowl in stories
gobble up whoever
- Cinderella
little Miss Muffet
and little Boy Blue,
Bo Peep's sheep
and Bo Peep too.
I never chew fairies
- I bolt them down,
Goldilocks and Mother Goose
though I retch at the feathers
and long golden hair
and when times are hard I have to make do
Old Mother Hubbard tough as they come
Tom Thumb
Jack Sprat
and serendipitous on the hill
Jack and Jill, concussed,
I gobble them up
and in her garden of shells and bells
contrary Mary
and Mary and her little lamb
- I wolf them down.
Snow White yum yum.